# INDEX

I0494693

## THANK YOU

I am able to write this book because of certain people in my life. My father, mother, sister and family for making me who I am.

My wife and son who has inspired me to do this and standing with me at every step.

So heartfelt thank you to all!

I am who I am is because of you all.

I dedicate this book to my son, Aarush.

## About AAR Consultancy

Singapore-based AAR Consultancy offers online marketing consultant services, solutions, expert guidance and staff training that delivers black and white positive results. Search engine optimization, AdWords, Social media, EDMs, strategy, eCommerce & more.

Have over 10 years of experience. Managed campaigns and / or worked for **Streetdirectory**, **MDIS**, **Ogilvy - Unilever, Nestle, IBM, Guinness, Cathay, SingTel**, **American Express**, **Mothercare** and more.

I am an **MBA**, with **numerous** marketing and branding certifications including **Google AdWords**, **Analytics** and **Shopping** certification.

I have been featured on **Asian Entrepreneur Portals and Huffington Post** and also a tech contributor and writer for many site.

My clients for consultancy are SMEs in Singapore as for them every dollar spent is important. Many have vendors managing their campaign, my role is to wear their cap, be their guardian and ensure campaigns & vendors are delivering results as it should be.

In training too, I have been empowering individuals and corporates alike. I work with NTUC Learning and Conversion Hub – A SPH Associate Company for corporate training besides my own training classes

## About the Author

I would say when I was way younger I had a good pampered life. My mother a housewife, father worked in a Bank, sister was studious so she eventually went to USA on a scholarship and a scientist there now. They really pampered me growing up. I would say didn't know what was good and bad too much.

I committed several huge mistakes in life due to my naivety, including almost running away from home. In 2006 I came to Singapore, with house mortgaged, $100,000 in debt to complete my graduation at a ripe age of 25. Studying and sitting in class with other students 6-7 years younger. To add to pressure of succeeding, my dad was over 60 years, a service man & retired then. For both my bachelor and master I took loan. My parents, sister and later on my brother in law all helped me at that stage.

Fast forward to 10 years later, having gone through death of closed ones, an accident that almost took my wife away from me, battling finances and health, I now own a house, have a beautiful wife, Neesha and an awesome son, Aarush. I would say, parents, sister & god has been my guide, wife my support and my son my inspiration. In-fact having such a beautiful gift – my son, has been the turning point in my life. I have been very ably supported by my in-laws too, every time I needed them. Lucky to have family always by my side.

Still remember, my wife took so much of the financial pressure on her, looked after our son, while I slogged day and night to get this company standing on its feet. Even when I came to Singapore to study, she had a choice of not being with me knowing the financial burden I came with, knowing how much I would have to fight and struggle, but she stayed on, helping me emotionally, financially and any ways possible.
Wouldn't say things are awesome, but yes it's on its way!

Every struggle has made me more determined to succeed and help companies honestly and sincerely.

My vision, "Every dollar earned is so important, there shouldn't be a scenario where clients spend more than what they get, I want to help clients get more knowledgeable and make wise decisions for their online marketing strategy. AAR is the first 3 alphabets of my son's name, I wouldn't tarnish it and delivery only top quality work. My objective, your success"

# Why I chose to write this book

As a consultant, I have seen so many companies trying to conquer the online space, especially social media.

The most common mistake they do is to decide themselves what needs to go out.
They do not do ample research and listening to understand what their fans, followers and community wants. We need to be aware and realize that these are real people, at the other end of the computer. Their moods change, their day maybe good one day, bad the other, how they consume data differs, so there is no, 1 fixed formula for them and one should always have ears on the ground to understand what they want and cater to it.

**Yes, it's not easy, but if you are not ready to do it, my advice don't do it at all.**

Moreover, a large number of companies hire vendors to do their marketing. I am not saying all, but many of them have to survive too, so they do campaigns that utilize client budgets faster and that means more commission earnings for them. They do not always show the real picture. I am consultant of so many clients and have seen this so many times. Worst part is that the clients do not even know it.

Companies have to wake up and realize that, every dollar they spend is important and should have a return on it. They should be aware of what their vendors are doing and challenge them if required to get desired results.

I hope to educate companies and marketers and even if they could take away a teeny weeny bit from reading this, I would have done my part.

Towards the end I have outlined how some other media strategies can be used to get an effective campaign roll out with great returns.

## How to read this book?

Read this book like a strategy. I am writing this as if I am writing this for a company. A lot can be understood from that.

All views are mine and tried to bring in a flow in my first humble attempt of writing a book.

Please excuse me if you feel I haven't lived up to being an author and any feedback or contact appreciated at Soumik@aaronline.sg.

## Group Strategies for big group of companies

This part is always the beginning. All your strategy and branding has to be set at a group level. Group Strategy for Facebook, can be broken down in to the two components. Organic communication & promotion – Community Management or Paid communication – Facebook Ads.
***Also to be noted, all Facebook properties, for a group should follow the brand guidelines during their conversations or ads on Social media irrespective of countries.***

# Facebook Page / Community Management

This section contains some guidelines for naming or distinguishing pages and what types of posts you should put up in your pages. The views below are not reflective of anyone else, but what I have learnt from running campaigns for multiple industries, companies and countries.

- Naming Convention for different companies should be appended without any underscore "_" or hyphen "-".
  Example. Company in Australia should "XYZ AU", India would be "XYZ PH" and so forth for easy reference and recall power.
  You have to know who your target audience is. So based on that your **tonality** should be adhered to. Tonality should be in a manner that your company is there to help solve whatever fan's issue or problem is, make their life easier. This way user will trust and engage faster.
- Effort should be taken to engage community. A highly engaged community will eventually lead to lower advertising cost.
- Incentives should be given to fans for sharing info, images etc. This should promote healthy ownership of the page and community.
- For ease of engagement, communications should be divided into regular schedules for posts on Facebook Page
- Communication should be divided into broader channels. Communication guidelines mentioned here should be same for every property irrespective of country.

- **Frequency** of Posts Should not be more than 3-4 times a day.
- First post should be scheduled at 8:30 am – 9:30 am. Statistics have shown people use social media a lot during commuting to work hours. Also based on the buying behavior of your community you can later modify the times.
- There should be one point of contact (centralized contact) for the Facebook page and any post, revisions etc. should be done through this person to have better control on the posting.
- Weekends **should not** contain product, marketing or sales related post unless necessary. Should have fun posts, or better Articles or inspirational quotes.
- Weekends Should not be more than 1 or two posts. And as people tend to wake up early 10am or 11am is best suited for it.
- All conversations should be planned beforehand, and should follow a fixed format (Conversation Calendar) unless there is an emergency news or postings to be made.
- During morning, users tend to consume comparatively more of brand related posts. Posts about brands or events, promotions etc. This also gives them more time throughout the day to take action.
- Post lunch and evening/night community related posts (tips, event photos, guides, fun posts) work best.
- If there is an image that is to be posted and intention could be to promote it, pls ensure it follows the 20% rule for Facebook. As long as text is 20% of below in the image it would work. But as a general rule always maintain that ratio for all

images. You can check it with this tool: https://www.facebook.com/ads/tools/text_overlay See example below.

- Both types should be mixed and one shouldn't outweigh the other to have a good engaged community.
- Videos should feature regularly (at least 2-3 times) during the week. Length of video should not be more than 1 minute and should have interesting start to hold onto attention. Many companies fall in to the trap of having an elaborate introduction in the beginning, which should be avoided if possible.

⚠ Image text: **Low**
Your advert's reach may be slightly lower.

You may reach fewer people because there's too much text in the advert image. Facebook prefers advert images with little or no text. Consider changing your image before placing your order.

Mom 'N' Kids

- **Question & enquiries** should be answered within 24 hours. During weekend Auto-Responder should be set.

## Sample Conversation Calendar

| Category | Mon | Tues | Wed | Thu | Fri | Sat | Sun |
|---|---|---|---|---|---|---|---|
| Branding | 8:30am : Post | | 10 pm: Post | 8:30 am: Post | 3pm: Post | | |
| Products /Services 2 | | 3pm: Post | 8:30 am: Post | | | | |
| Events | 3pm: Post | | | | | | |
| Fun Related post | | 8:30 am: Post | 3 pm: post | 10pm: Post | 8:30 am: Post | | |
| Quotes or inspiratio nal | | | | | | | 10 am : Post |
| Articles | 10pm: Post | | | | 10 pm: Post | 10 am : Post | |

A conversation calendar needs to be written and finalized with posts and images by the previous week.

Best way to effectively manage time is to schedule the posts, but keep checking on comments and feedback if given by community.

# POST EXAMPLES

**Eg: of Articles. Doesn't always have to be from the Brand.**
Your community is made up for real people. So do not be afraid to seed in content that may not be of your brand but relevant to the target audience of your community.

For example a baby clothes retailer, or people from kids industry may put up a post like that.

It's normal - we all make mistakes!

## 10 Reasons You Shouldn't Worry About Making Mistakes As A Mother

It's truly amazing how prepared you can be for parenthood, only to have everything you thought you know fall by the proverbial wayside. For me, it took about six...

ROMPER.COM | BY GLYNIS RATCLIFFE

**Fun or feel good post can be as simple as this.**

A good way to push brand with a real life event of PSLE exams in Singapore. Brand retention is highest in these. Better way to portray brand then just pushing the product.

To all students taking your PSLE Science paper, may the forces be with you! #NeverGiveUp #MILO

Quotes Example. Can be down easily in-house. You can create a trend with these, that people can use or look forward to.

CEO Speaks:

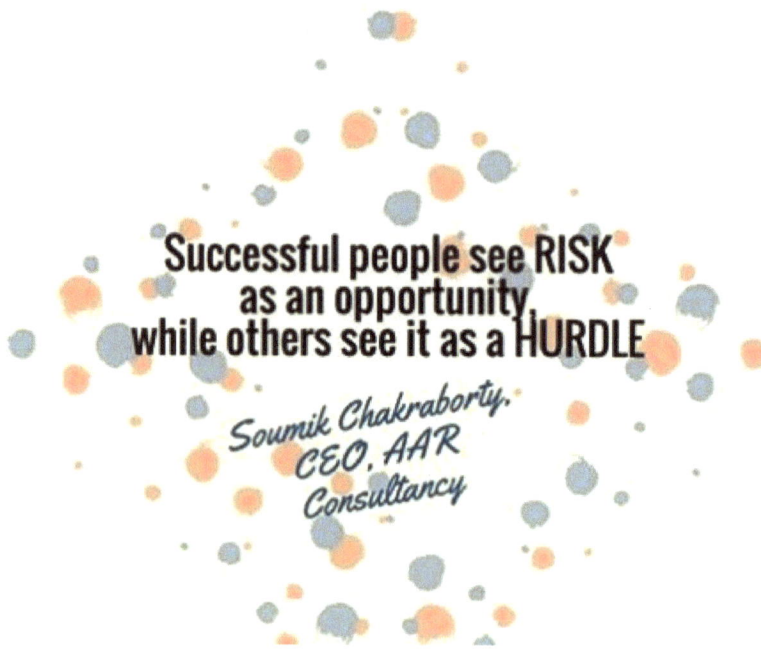

Successful people see RISK
as an opportunity,
while others see it as a HURDLE

Soumik Chakraborty,
CEO, AAR
Consultancy

## Facebook Ads

- All ads that is run anywhere should be for lead generation and tracked through pixels.
- I am not very fond of branding ads. How do you measure branding? How can you say what is your branding for an ad as compared to your competitor and how dos branding help w.r.t in terms of sales?
- A good converting ad would do better and automatically elevate your branding. So all ads must have a conversion in mind.
- First step is to ensure all Facebook Pixels and Google Analytics codes are added in on the website including the "thank you" page that a user sees after he or she has sent in an enquiry or performed a pre-set action. Ad vendor can assist in doing that.
- Targeting is most important for Facebook Ads.
- Besides interest and other targeting, parental targeting is very important if you can equate your audience based on that. By doing this you are able to target parents of children similar to your target market.
- Ad Headlines should have direct statement of what user will get from your brand. Which may be elaborated in the ad copy. If there is a promotion, should be mentioned at headlines. Link Description should have bragging rights, or other awards if any.
- Multiple visual and copy testing is advised for an ad set. Not more than 3.
  Testing should be done on the following components
    i. Visual
    ii. Headline – Best Offer or a solution to problem your target audience has

iii.   Ad Body – Giving a teaser to solve the problem, or why should they contact you.

iv.   Link description. Usually 2-3 lines. Not max. Place for bragging rights

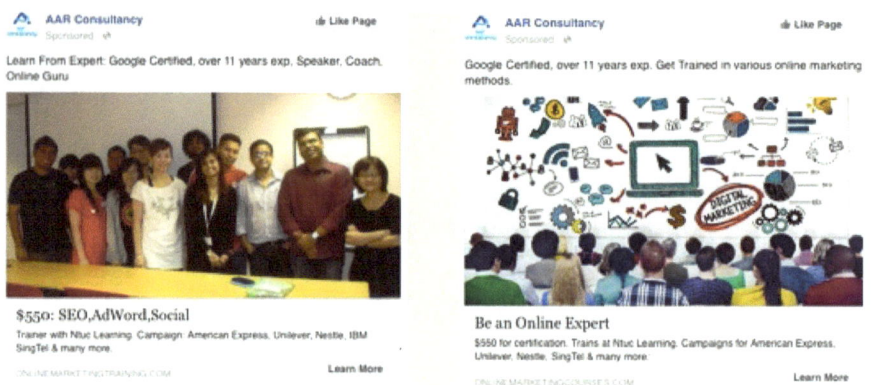

- Look Alike Audience Modeling. It is an underdog and people do not know about it. NEW CAMPAIGNS SHOULD start only after doing this or its money been wasted. There is a way in Facebook where you can target people who are most likely to buy your products and services and are similar to your customers. Saves hundreds of dollars and lets you target them elimination broader audience. For Lookalike and pixels please contact me at Soumik@aaronline.sg. I will teach you for free but didn't put it here as it can't be taught through screenshots.
- Ads should have at least 2% CTR. Relevancy should be more than 7 and high positive impact. It's not an either or. All of these should be present for it to be cost effective and give more conversion.
- Ensure that CPM value should not increase $2.

- Cost per click or CTR cost per click should be low. It can go up to $0.20 or $0.25 cents, which is still considered high. But should be close to or less than $0.20 cents. The lower the better.

| Rel... | Clicks (A.. | CTR.. | CPC (All) | Pos... | Neg... |
|---|---|---|---|---|---|
| 9 | 2.568 | 3.84% | $0.07 | High | Low |
| | 2.568<br>Total | 3.84%<br>Per Imp | $0.07<br>Per Click | | |

- Facebook has tied up with shutter stock and really good quality images are available to be used for ads for free. Some of them are quite good and many types available. Some of them could be used to try out ad serving.

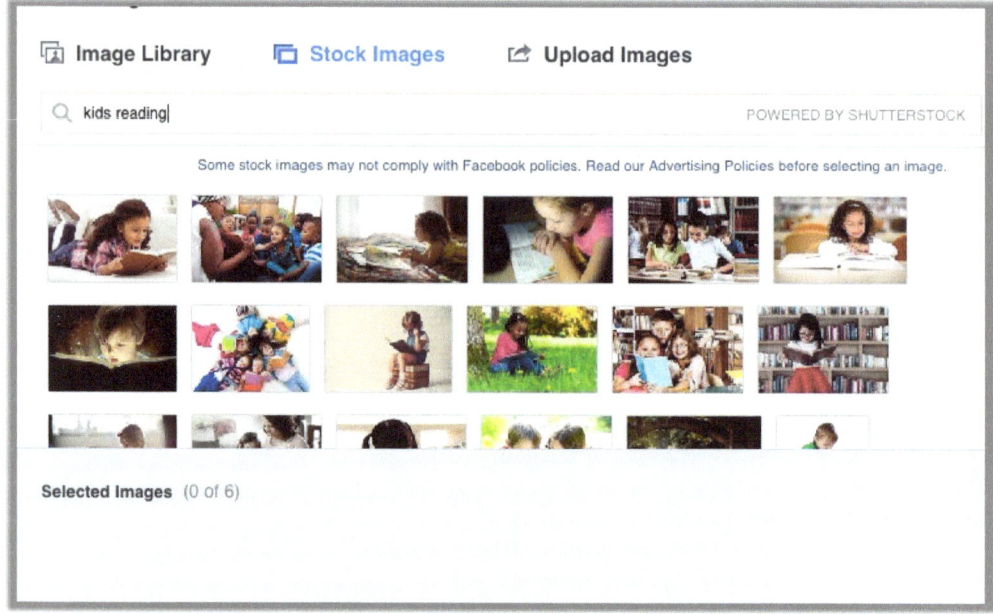

FREE shutter stock images for your ads. Just search for a product, phrase or service and it shows you options.

## Steps to Create Facebook Ads

1> Goto Create Ads From your Facebook Home Page

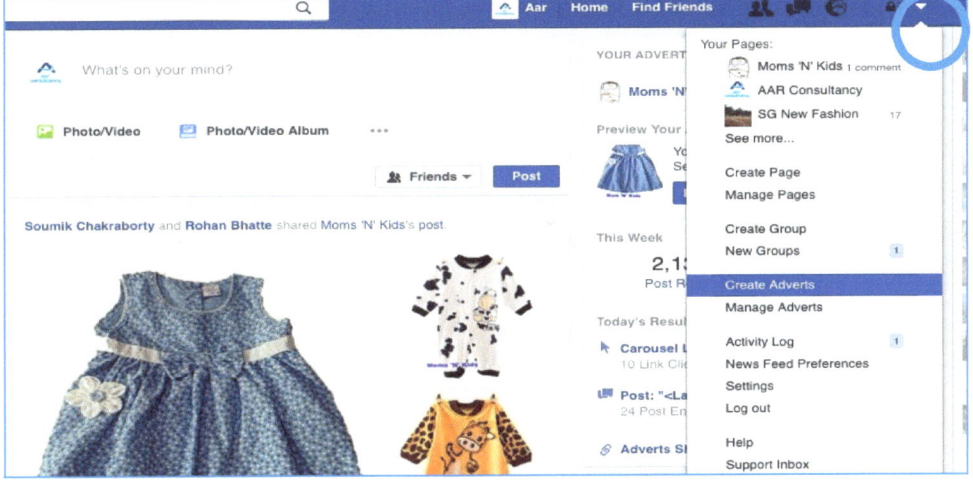

## 2> Select Objective of your ad campaign

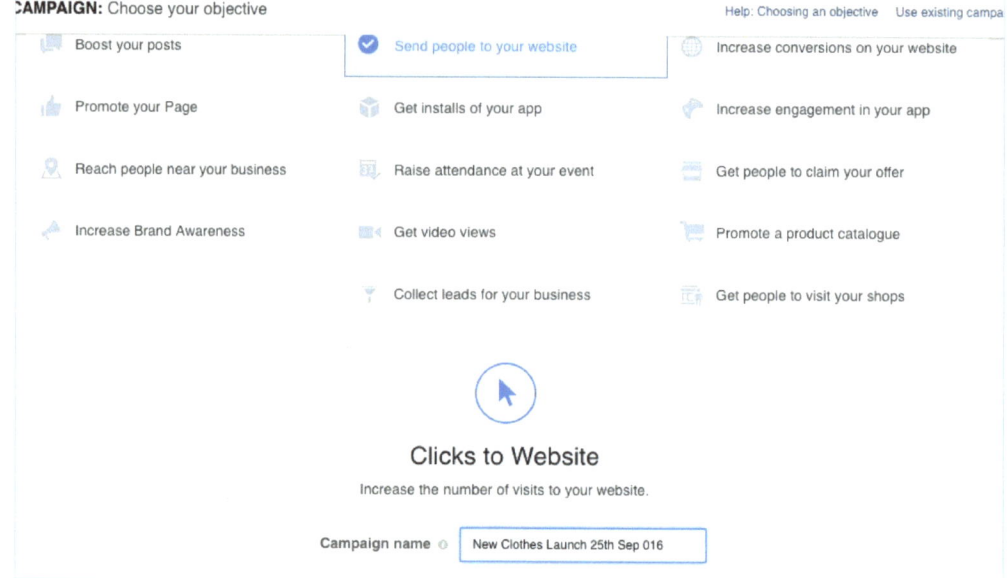

Give your campaign a name. Make sure your campaign is such, that looking at the name you can decipher what that campaign was. It's for your reference

3> Audience and targeting. Very important stage. Facebook will keep showing your estimated audience as you add or delete your targeting criteria.

You can either select based on Facebook browse of categories or search and see whether your phrase is available.

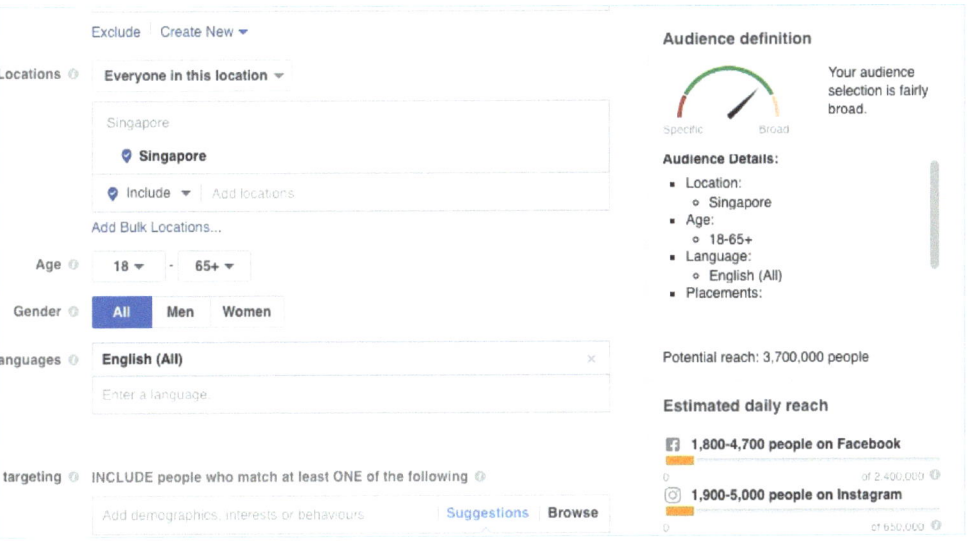

a> Using own search phrase

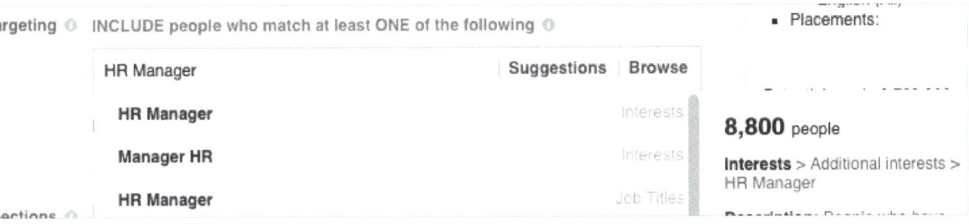

Be mindful if I want to target people who are HR Mgrs, I will select the option with "Job Titles" if I want to target who are interested in HR Mgrs I will select "Interests" and so on.

    a. Using Facebook Browse

A wide variety of categories are present and you can browse and select as required. It's even as detailed as finding and targeting parenting levels. Just browse and you would be surprise to see what you may find.

| tailed targeting ⓘ | INCLUDE people who match at least ONE of the following ⓘ | |
|---|---|---|
| | Add demographics, interests or behaviours | Suggestions   Browse |
| | ▸   Home | |
| | ▸   Life events | |
| | ▾   Parents | |
| Connections ⓘ | ▾    All Parents | |
| |      (0-12 months) New Parents | ☐ |
| |      (01-02 Years) Parents with Toddlers | ☐ |
| |      (03-05 Years) Parents with Preschoolers | ☐ |
| |      (06–08 years) Parents with early school-age children | ☐ |
| ts | | |
| adverts to the right pe |      (08-12 Years) Parents with Preteens | ☐ |

4> Placements

Tells you where your ads would be seen.

One suggestion I would give. Instagram is more suited for lifestyle, teens, food, clothes etc. If you are marketing products that doesn't fit into any of them, try and stay away from Instagram. You may get response but at a higher cost.

Automatic Placements (recommended)

Your adverts will automatically be shown to your audience in the places where they're likely to perform best. For this objective, placements may include Facebook, Instagram and Audience Network. Learn more.

- **Edit Placements**

Removing placements may reduce the number of people you reach and may make it less likely that you'll meet your goals. Learn more.

| | | |
|---|---|---|
| Device types | All devices (recommended) ▼ | |
| Platforms ▼ | Facebook | ✓ |
| | Feeds | ✓ |
| | Right column | ✓ |
| | Instagram | ✓ |
| | Audience Network | ✓ |

**ADVANCED OPTIONS**

Specific mobile devices & operating systems

Exclude categories for Audience Network

Apply block lists for the Audience Network

## 5> Budgets

You can set daily or lifetime budget. Personally I prefer setting daily, as it lets me control my spend and I provide start and end days. You can optimize for clicks or conversion but do not do it for impression. Tends to be more expensive and not that effective.

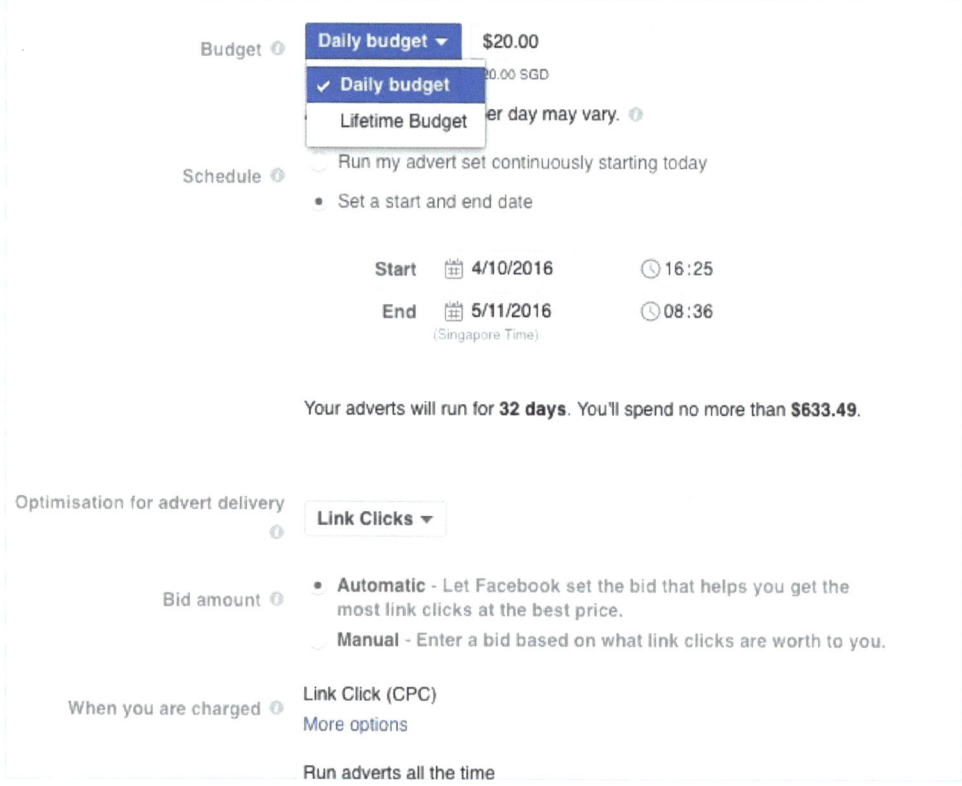

6> Format Tells you what kind of Ad Unit it is?

a. Carousel – Collection of images
b. Single Image. Single ad
c. Video
d. Slideshow

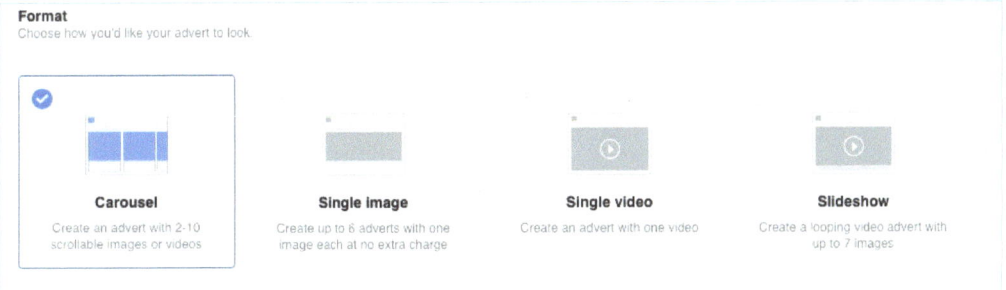

To get FREE shutter stock images, click single image and click Free stock images.

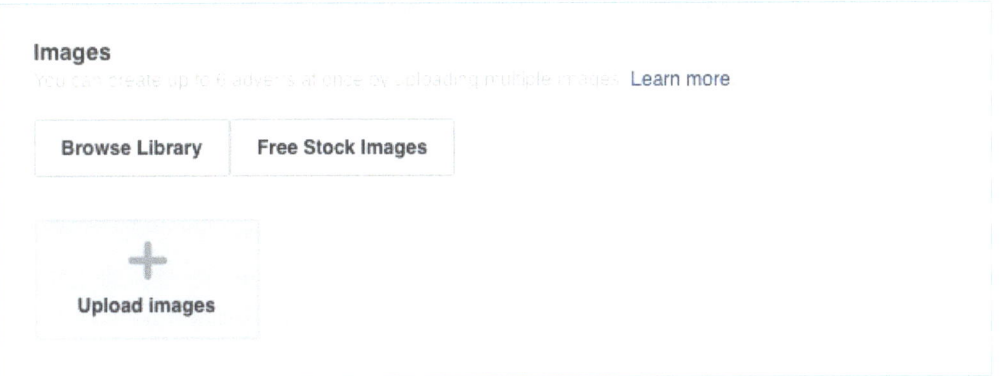

Free Stock Images

Based on your query you would see free images to be used. Alternatively, you can upload images from your pc too.

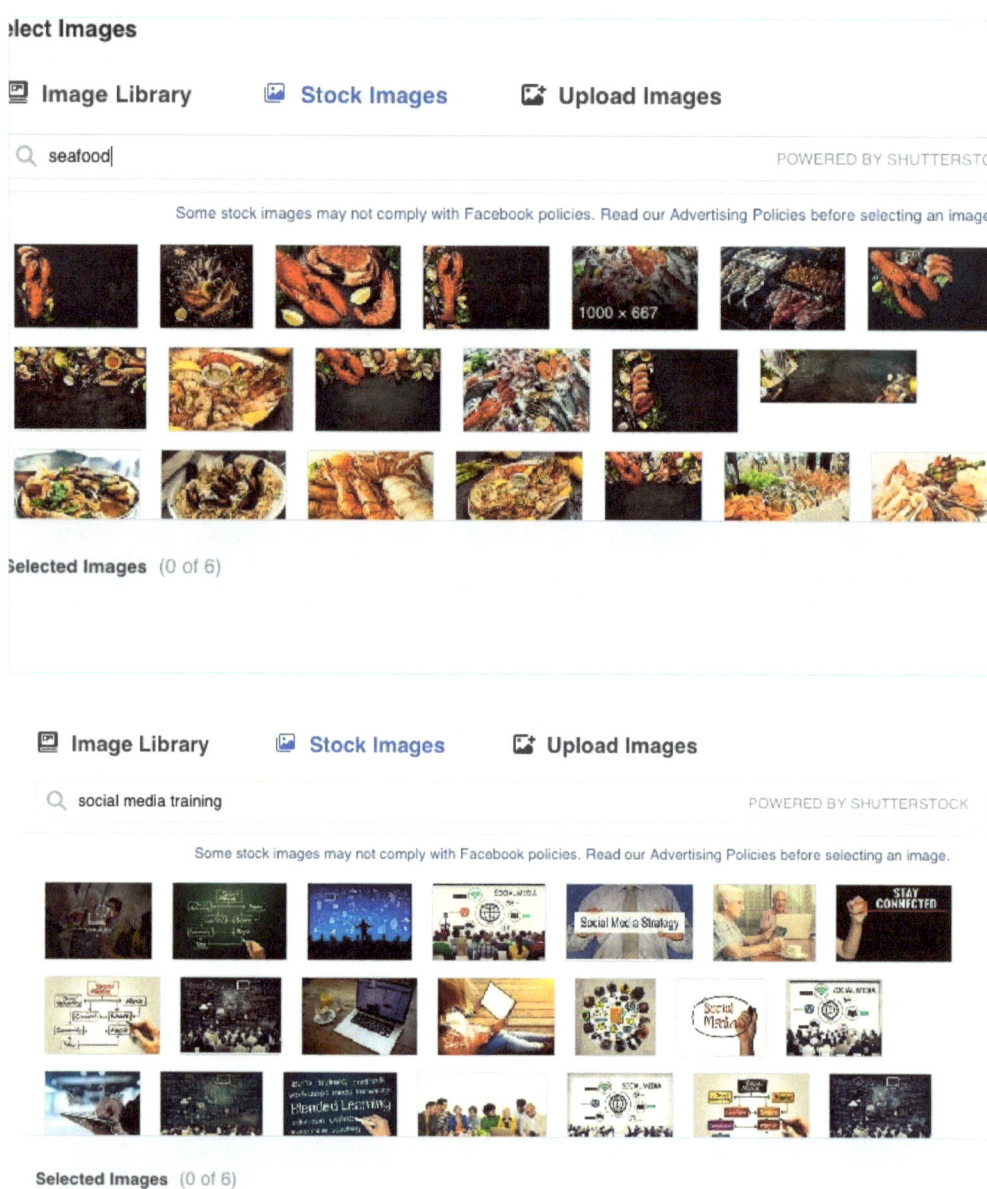

7> Images, Links, Ad copies

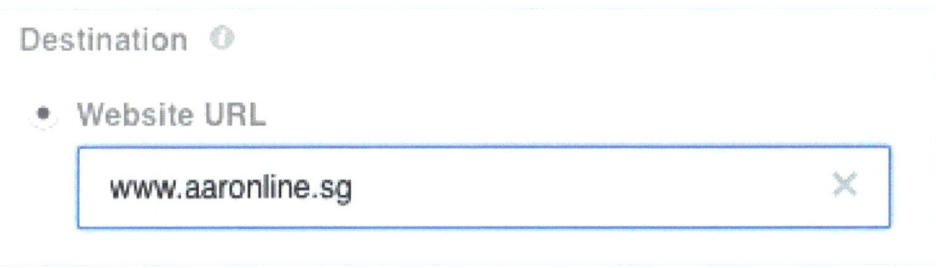

Destination ⓘ

● Website URL

www.aaronline.sg                                    ✕

Type in your ad copies and headlines based on guidelines
given earlier and select your call to action button accordingly.

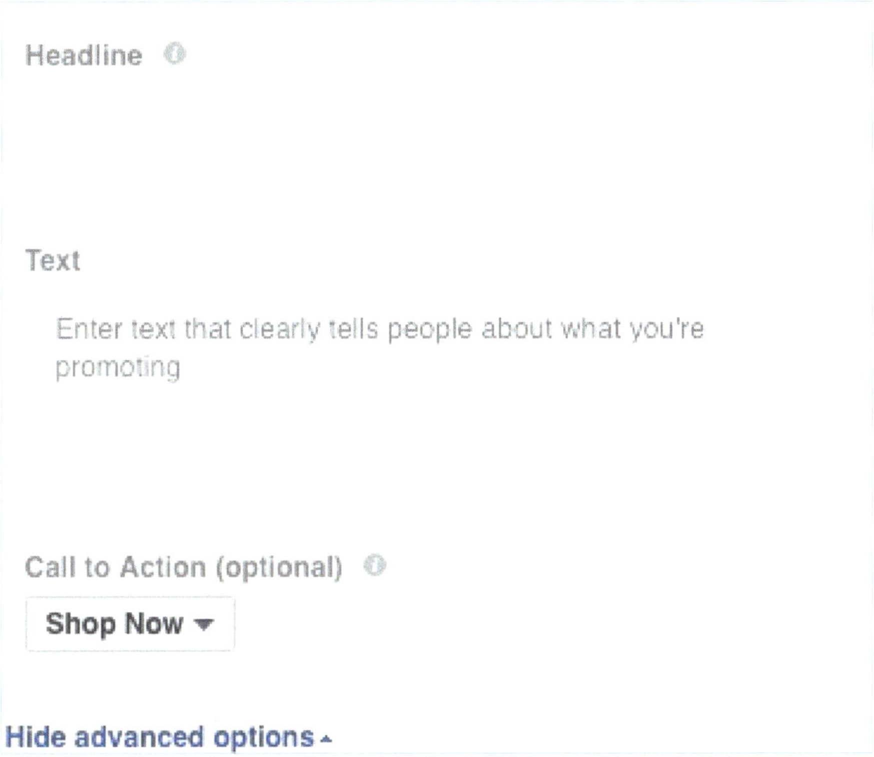

Headline ⓘ

Text

Enter text that clearly tells people about what you're
promoting

Call to Action (optional) ⓘ

Shop Now ▼

**Hide advanced options** ▲

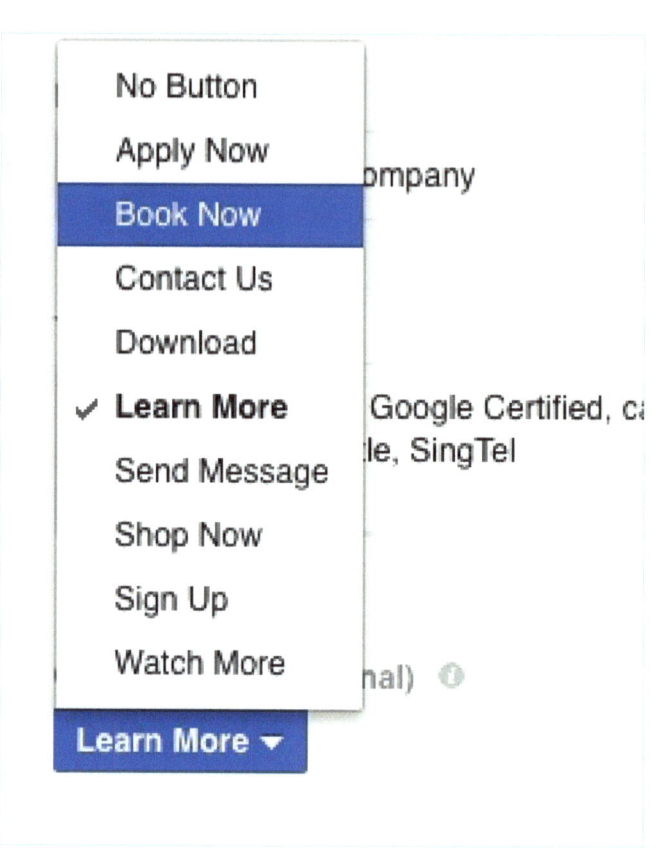

8> When everything is done. You need to see how ad looks on the right hand side of your page and click on Place Order

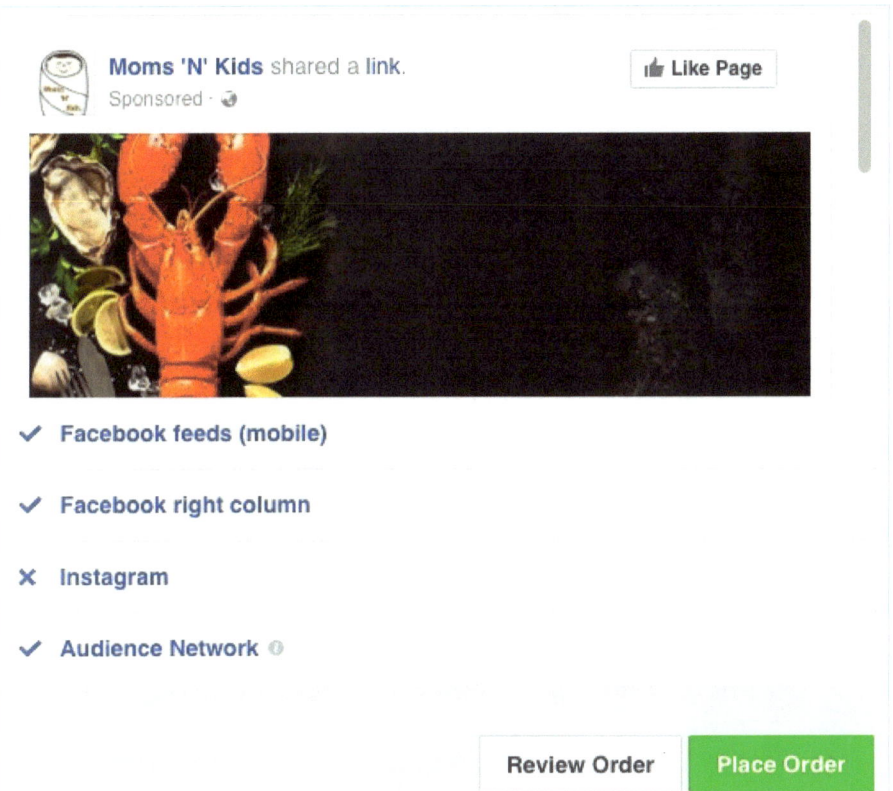

## Social Media Crisis Management

Main Principal of Crisis Management is:
Listen > Convince > Convert

- As mentioned before response and replies need to be given out within 24 hours. That would mean constant monitoring of social media platforms. Many companies would say that we do not have time or too much work. Well my answer, this needs to happen, monitoring needs to be detailed, so if the company is serious enough they would have to find ways doing it.
- If the page has more than 20-30k fans with engagement rate of 10% and above (good metric) you should have a team of community management personnel (1-3). Their jobs are to comb your platform (just the page would do for a start), listen to sentiments & what their community is saying.
- **First and most IMPORTANT Rule** for a negative comment or complain posted on your page is :::

- DO NOT and I REPEAT: DO NOT delete negative comments or complaints.
- If someone has taken the time and effort to come onto your page and vent out, the least you can do is listen. Try to understand what prompted them to do that post and see how you can help them, convince them you care and show it through your action. In doing so you would have converted another user to

your loyal groups. And If the entire community can see that, it has a very powerful positive multiplying impact.

- Follow these steps in case of crisis, complains or negative posts.

    i.    Your First Objective is to let everyone know, you have listened, you understand and want to set it right, irrespective of whether it may or may not be your fault.

    ii.    With that in mind, move the conversation out of the community wall on Facebook to the private messages(PM). Everyone doesn't need to see the exchanges. You can ask them to call someone, email someone or once in PM mode can ask for their contact.
*Sample Post: "Hello Mr/Ms X, we are very sorry for the inconvenience and trouble <mention issue> has caused you. We have messaged you privately, as we want to sort this out asap for you. Please do reply back to us through private messages so we can start action in it."*
You may also direct them to an email or number. *"You may call Mr Z on xxxx-xxxx or email him at ss@ss.com and we would get on it right away. Rest assured solving, this for you is out utmost priority.*
But ideally get theirs, because they are already irate, and if response through email is not immediate or no one picks up phone, it may make the situation worse.

    iii.    Look at the tonality. It doesn't say it's your fault, but you empathize and want to sort it out. But once you start communicating with the irate user, then analyze the issued and do sort it out.

iv. Once issue is resolved and customer is happy. Go back to the original public post and add on to replying, you are sorry for the inconvenience that was caused to the user and you were glad that your company could sort out the matter to the users liking. Shows the world you listened and solved it.

v. If it's an error of really high proportion like big mistake, or unfortunately something unforsaken happened in your office brand involving consumers, best way is for your "Top Management" issuing press release (best if it's a video) and apologizing straight up. People do appreciate companies that own up to the mistake and takes steps to prevent future ones.

## Strategy for Other Media

A.⬚.1.  Google AdWords should be a part of every strategy. It is comparatively more expensive, so initially as a start, suggestion would be to use Facebook more, as potential customers can be reached faster through that. Ad extensions like telephone numbers or promotions should definitely be added. Historically, telephone numbers have proved to be effective as users can directly call you without going through process of clicking on to site, browsing, filling lead and waiting passively. This will also help prevent some clicks and benefit in cost savings, and you will still get leads calling in.

A.⬚.2.  GDN (Google Display Network) should be used for "re-marketing" - using visitors that have already visited the site. So in order to ensure GDN and other campaigns are successful, targeting for initial campaigns becomes even more important.

A.⬚.3.  For GDN, interest, topics, placements all must be used diligently.

A.⬚.4.  GSP, Gmail/Google sponsored promotions must be tried on. These days gradually GSP is picking up very well. Attractive visual, direct benefits statements and lead generation form all can be utilized to get good results through Gsps.

A.⬚.5.  Proper Marketing Strategy would be:

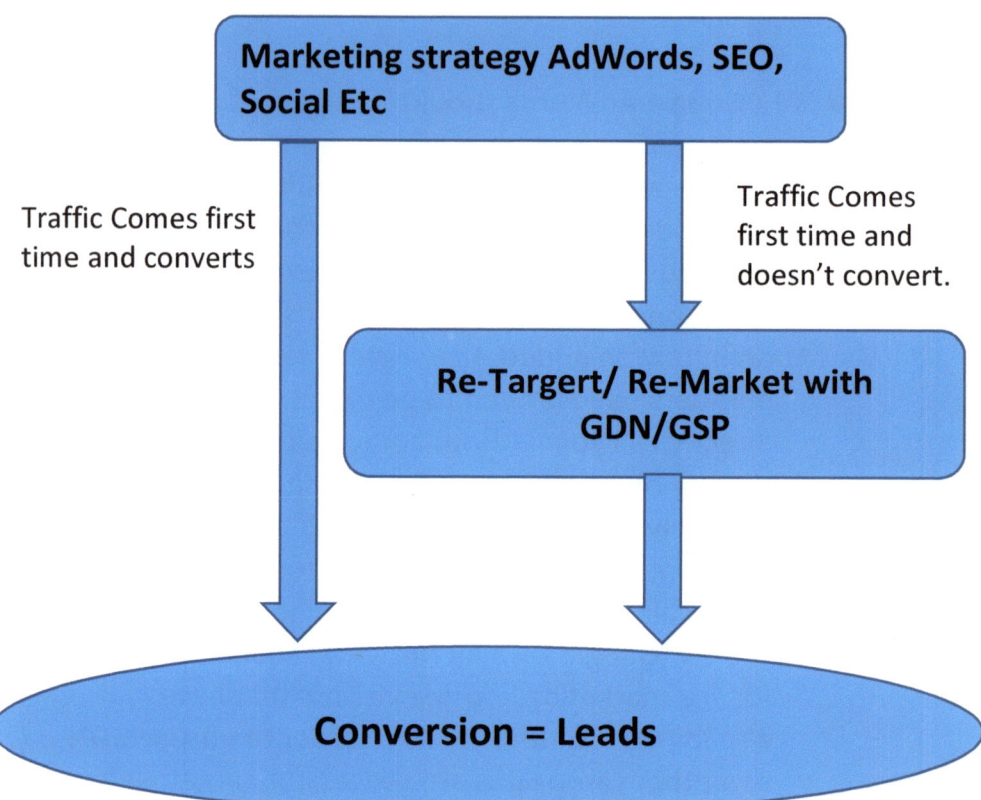

# FAQ "Frequently Asked Questions"

- **How is the document outlined?**

  The document outlines a Group strategy if relevant with respect to, communications and ads. All countries, branches must adhere to it. Sample good posts and ads screenshots provided.

- **Can the guidelines be followed hard – set and sure way to generate success?**

  The guidelines document is right called so, because it's a framework, suggestions and a guide. It involves AAR's and Soumik's 10 years of expertise running these type of ads. But we are dealing with consumers whose browsing pattern may change depending on mood, personal actions, current events etc. Ads and communications is something that is learnt new every day and should be tested to see what works best.
  But these guidelines have proven over time to work and this is a good place to start and as deeper understanding of your consumers are understood and analyzed, should be modified accordingly.

- **What is the best way to have content ownership and moderation for Social Media management?**

  There should be one point of contact who moderates and maintains a page. Prevents confusing user with multiple writing styles, multiple tonality and then who would action against comments, feedback becomes confusing as well. BEST is always to have a singular or centralized control.

- **If I have an agency doing my ads, what should I be wary off?**

  As mentioned above things like CTR > 2%, CPC cost less than $0.20, High positive intention and high relevancy. Just CTR and Cost is not enough. Along with it, number of conversions the ad generated **should** always be counted in. **PIXELS, LOOKALIKE are a MUST THESE DAYS.**

## Source of Information

Most of the ideas and work expressed are from my experience of running campaigns for various industries and companies.

One reference was taken from Milo Singapore Facebook page for showcasing fun post used in a relevant manner.

There shouldn't be any other issues but if any of you feel that content or images seems like your work and I may have used it without permission, please feel free to write to me at Soumik@aaronline.sg.

I have written everything from my knowledge but if it is indeed your work, we will discuss and either remove or give proper reference in next edition or whatever is decided.

www.ingramcontent.com/pod-product-compliance
Lightning Source LLC
Chambersburg PA
CBHW041144180526
45159CB00002BB/727